The Screaming Orgasm

69 X-Rated Cocktails

Kirsten Amann

RUNNING PRESS
PHILADELPHIA · LONDON

© 2012 by Kirsten Amann
Photography © 2012 by Allan Penn

A Hollan Publishing, Inc. Concept

Credits
Page 68: French Kiss was adapted from a recipe by Audrey Saunders, owner of Pegu Club, New York
Page 92: Wet Spot was adapted from a recipe by Willy Shine and Aisha Sharpe, mixologists at Bed, New York

Published by Running Press,
A Member of the Perseus Books Group

Books published by Running Press are available at special discounts for bulk purchases in the United States by corporations, institutions, and other organizations. For more information, please contact the Special Markets Department at the Perseus Books Group, 2300 Chestnut Street, Suite 200, Philadelphia, PA 19103, or call (800) 810-4145, ext. 5000, or e-mail special.markets@perseusbooks.com.

ISBN 978-0-7624-4307-9
Library of Congress Control Number: 2011933257

E-book ISBN 978-0-7624-4506-6

9 8 7 6 5 4 3 2 1
Digit on the right indicates the number of this printing

Cover and interior design by Corinda Cook
Edited by Jordana Tusman
Typography: Aviano, Copperplate, Franklin Gothic, Helvetica Neue, Kepler, Latienne, Madison, Odette, and Samantha

Running Press Book Publishers
2300 Chestnut Street
Philadelphia, PA 19103-4371

Visit us on the web!
www.runningpresscooks.com

Contents

Hooking Up 46

Hot and Heavy 72

All the Way 102

One-Night Stand 124

The Walk of Shame 148

Sex and cocktails mix well together. They always have, which may be why there are scores of drinks with sexually suggestive names: Between the Sheets or Hanky Panky, anyone? And then there are the drinks that are just downright dirty, like Deep Throat or Leg Spreader. From sexy starter cocktails to X-rated potations, this book includes a variety of racy drinks and tipples that titillate, whether you're looking to spice up a soiree, embarrass the bride-to-be at her bachelorette party, or have simply always wondered, "What exactly is a Sloe Comfortable Screw Against the Wall?"

The sixty-nine cocktails chosen to spice up your drinking regimen have all been grouped to mirror their explicit subject matter. Featuring cocktails like Dirty Virgin and Maiden's Blush, *Flirting* is dedicated to the drinks that help you light the spark. *Hooking Up* is a nod to what happens once you decide to take your mutual attraction a step further, with drinks like French Kiss and Hickey. The cocktails in *Hot and Heavy* are a salute to those of us who aren't afraid to get it on, with drinks like Bosom Caresser and Wet Spot. *All the Way* cuts right to the chase, with drinks like Climax and the infamous libation that lent its name to this book's title, the Screaming Orgasm. *One-Night Stand* is a whimsical homage to all the great, sexy things that can happen when you know you'll never see your lover again, such as Sex on the Beach and Strip and Go Naked. And when you're ready to dip into *The Walk of Shame*, which focuses on that triumphant march home wearing last night's cocktail dress and this morning's sexy bedroom hair, mix up some cocktails that will help ease your hangover, like Corpse Reviver and Afterglow Fizz.

We are lucky to be imbibing during a liquid renaissance, when great drinks made with fresh ingredients can be found in cocktail dens across the globe. The Screaming Orgasm is rarely serious or fussy, and neither is this book. The cocktails and shots included here were selected to inspire a bit of lighthearted fun and laughter at your next cocktail party or bar night out. Some, like the Angel's Tit, are time-tested classics born in the early twentieth century. Others

are of questionable parentage and dubious intentions but would certainly make a naughty bartender's ears perk up when ordered, like the bachelorette party staple, the legendary Blow Job.

These drinks have been sourced from far and wide and were hand-selected to make you blush or giggle as you consider ordering them. Mix them up at home or order them while out on the town, if you dare. Whatever you do, don't take these drinks, or yourself, too seriously. This is no place to be shy. Whether you're in the mood for a little Sex on the Beach or ready to dive in head-first with Screaming Orgasm, this book is your go-to guide to sixty-nine of the sexiest

Cocktail Essentials

Before you start

stirring and shaking your X-rated cocktails, it would be useful to stock your home bar with some basic cocktail essentials. What follows is a list of key glassware, indispensable tools, quick syrup recipes, a spirits glossary, and much more. With these tips in your cocktail arsenal, you will be well on your way to enjoying your next Screaming Orgasm, or even Over-the-Pants Hand Job, right in the comfort of your own home.

Glassware

Cocktail or Martini Glass: A stemmed glass with a cone-shaped bowl over a flat base. Classic and vintage cocktail glasses can take various forms, from shallow, wide-mouthed coupes to fancy glasses with square edges and anything in between.

Collins Glass: A tall, narrow glass used for serving drinks over ice and topped with soda. The narrow glass keeps soda fizzy.

Old-Fashioned or Rocks Glass: A short, wide glass used for drinks served with ice, or spirits enjoyed neat. This is often called an old-fashioned glass after the iconic drink that is served in it.

Highball Glass: Similar to a collins glass but wider. Also used for drinks served over ice and topped with soda.

Shot Glass: A small glass that typically holds about two ounces of liquid.

Tools

Bar Spoon: A long-handled spoon used by bartenders to mix stirred cocktails. May also be used to measure out ingredients, as it holds about the size of a teaspoon.

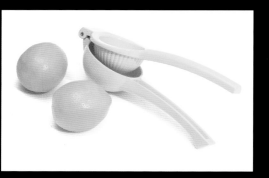

Citrus Squeezer: A tool designed to squeeze the juice from one half of a lemon or lime. A great addition to your kitchen!

Boston Shaker: The bartender's choice for shaking cocktails for well over one hundred years, the Boston shaker consists of a pint glass and a metal shaker tin that covers the mixing glass to create a perfect seal.

Hawthorne Strainer: A strainer outfitted with a semicircular spring that fits snugly inside the shaker tin as you pour out its contents.

Channel Knife: A short knifelike tool with a metal tooth used to carve citrus

Muddler: A sturdy tool, resembling a pestle, used to press ingredients to extract juices and oils in the bottom of a glass.

Jigger: A two-sided tool used to measure ingredients for cocktails.

Julep Strainer: A spoon-shaped strainer perforated with fine holes that fits snugly into a mixing glass to keep fine bits of ice out of

Simple Syrups

Grenadine Syrup: Homemade grenadine is more delicious by leaps and bounds than the preservative-packed store-bought stuff. It's essentially pomegranate simple syrup. Combine equal parts (1 cup unsweetened pomegranate juice to 1 cup sugar) in a saucepan, bring to a boil, and stir to dissolve. Reduce the heat and simmer for 7 minutes, or until thick enough to coat a spoon. Cover the saucepan, allow the syrup to cool, and bottle it. This will keep for up to 1 month, if refrigerated.

Honey Syrup: Combine equal parts (1 cup honey to 1 cup water) in a saucepan, bring to a boil, and stir to dissolve. Reduce the heat and simmer for 7 minutes, or until thick enough to coat a spoon. Cover the saucepan, allow the syrup to cool, and bottle it. This will keep for up to 1 month, if refrigerated.

Passion Fruit Syrup: Combine 1 cup water, 1 cup sugar, and ½ cup passion fruit pulp (you can buy frozen at the grocery store) in a small saucepan. Bring to a boil over medium-high heat, stirring until the sugar dissolves. Reduce the heat and simmer for 15 minutes. Cover the saucepan, allow the syrup to cool, and bottle it. This will keep for up to 2 weeks, if refrigerated.

Raspberry/Blackberry/Strawberry Syrup: Combine 1 pint of fresh or frozen desired berries, 1 cup sugar, and 1 cup water in a small saucepan. Bring to a boil, and stir to dissolve, crushing the berries as you work. Cover the saucepan and allow the syrup to cool. Strain through a fine mesh strainer to remove the skin and seeds, and then bottle it. This will keep for up to 2 weeks, if refrigerated.

Simple Syrup: Essentially just sugar and water, simple syrup can be made a few ways. The easiest is to combine equal parts of each (1 cup sugar to 1 cup water) in a small saucepan, bring to a boil, and stir to dissolve. Cover the saucepan, allow the syrup to cool, and bottle it. This will keep for up to 1 month, if refrigerated.

Spicy Syrup: Combine 2 sliced jalapeños, 2 tablespoons Korean chili flakes, and 2 tablespoons black peppercorns with 1 cup sugar and 1 cup water and simmer, stirring to dissolve the sugar. Remove from the heat, cover the saucepan, and allow the syrup to cool. Allow the ingredients to sit until the desired spiciness is achieved. Strain the ingredients and bottle it. The syrup should keep for up to 1 month, if refrigerated.

Mixology

Here are a few suggestions and rules of thumb to guarantee success as you mix up some sultry cocktails.

Dry Shaking: When working with eggs in cocktails, always combine the ingredients in a mixing glass without ice and shake for twenty seconds to emulsify the ingredients. Add ice to the shaker and continue to shake vigorously. Shake egg drinks long and hard to achieve a beautiful layer of foam on top.

Flaming Citrus Peels: Flaming a citrus peel is a very cool party trick. Cut a small circle of citrus peel about the size of a quarter from a firm, fresh fruit. Oranges tend to work well. Try to avoid cutting the pith with the peel. Light a match or ignite your lighter. Pick up the citrus peel, holding it by the edges between your thumb and forefinger. Hold the match or lighter above your cocktail and the citrus peel above the flame. Snap the twist quickly, expelling citrus oil from the skin. The oils will ignite in a quick, brilliant flash.

Flaming Cocktails: Turn up the heat—literally—on your cocktail by setting it on fire. This is another very cool party trick that will caramelize the flavors of the alcohol in your drink. Layer your liquor of choice (anything 80 proof or higher will ignite) over your cocktail by pouring the spirit over the back of a bar spoon that's touching the side of the glass. Once the alcohol has settled, apply a flame to the top of the drink, either with a long lighter or a match. Your guests will be mesmerized by the blue flame.

Fresh is Best: Good cocktails are literally the sum of their parts! Use freshly squeezed juice or homemade syrups whenever possible to guarantee delicious results. Find homemade simple syrup recipes on page 12. You should also use the freshest eggs you can find when making cocktails with egg whites or yolk. Cocktails made with eggs are less common nowadays, but there was a time when they were considered a common ingredient in the mixologist's arsenal. The alcohol and acid in most cocktails will kill most of the egg's dangerous bacteria, but you might consider using pasteurized eggs or egg products as alternatives.

Ice: Use fresh ice and plenty of it when mixing cocktails, filling the mixing glass or shaker tin before chilling down your ingredients.

Layering: If a recipe calls for a cocktail to be layered, the ingredients should be layered according to the order listed.

Muddling: Combine ingredients in the bottom of a mixing glass and press with a muddler to extract juices or oils.

Shaking vs. Stirring: Drinks that are made with just spirits, liqueurs, syrups, or bitters, and no citrus juice should be stirred. Shaking them will create air bubbles that lead to cloudy cocktails and a different feel on the palate. Save the shaking for drinks made with citrus.

Garnish

Cayenne Sugar Rim: To make a spicy rim for your cocktail glass, combine 1 to 2 teaspoons cayenne pepper (depending on how spicy you want the rim) with 1 to 3 tablespoons sugar. Wet the rim of the desired glass with a lime wedge, and then gently roll the rim of the glass in the mixture, moving the glass around until the rim is coated. Keep the glass upside down and give it a gentle shake to remove excess.

Citrus Twist: A long, thin twist of citrus peel made by pressing the tooth of a channel knife into the skin of the fruit and tracing it in a spiral around the fruit.

Lemon/Lime Wedge: Cut a lemon or lime in half and then slice each half into thirds or quarters, depending on the size of the fruit.

Maraschino Cherry: Stemmed red cherries that can be found in most grocery or liquor stores.

Sugar/Salt Rim: To rim a glass, spread a few tablespoons of sugar, salt, or other crushed ingredient on a small plate. Wet the sides and/or rim of the desired glass with a lime wedge, and then gently roll the sides and/or rim in the mixture, moving the glass around until all the sides or rim are coated. Keep the glass upside down and give it a gentle shake to remove excess.

Spirits Glossary

The following is a list of sexy spirits that are used in this book. It may be helpful to know that an aperitif is a drink that is served before a meal to stimulate the appetite, and a digestif is a drink that is served after a meal to aid digestion.

Absinthe: An anise-flavored spirit, named for its key ingredient Artemisia absinthium, or wormwood, which is toxic when consumed in large doses.

Amaretto: A sweet almond-flavored Italian liqueur.

Angostura Bitters: Aromatic bitters made in Trinidad and Tobago from a proprietary blend of herbs and spices.

Aperol: A bitter Italian aperitif made from orange peels, rhubarb, and gentian.

Applejack: American apple brandy.

Brandy: A spirit made from fermented fruits and by distilling wine.

Campari: A bitter Italian aperitif made from herbs and fruits that is bright red in color.

Chambord: A raspberry liqueur made in France.

Chartreuse: An herbal French liqueur made from a blend of 130 botanicals. Green Chartreuse is the original and is the liqueur from which the color takes its name. Yellow Chartreuse is made with honey and is considerably sweeter.

Cointreau: An orange-flavored aperitif.

Crème de Cacao: A chocolate-flavored liqueur sweetened with vanilla.

Crème de Violette: A floral French liqueur flavored with violets.

Curaçao: A colorless liqueur made from the dried peel of the laraha fruit. It is often given artifical coloring, like blue and orange, to add bright colors to cocktails.

Dubonnet: A wine-based aperitif made from herbs, spices, and fortified wine.

Fernet Branca: A bitter Italian digestif made from 27 proprietary herbs.

Galliano: A sweet yellow liqueur made from a blend of herbs and spices, with vanilla and anise overtones.

Genever: A distilled spirit made from malt wine and flavored with juniper and other botanicals. It's considered a precursor to modern-day gin.

Gin: A grain spirit flavored from juniper berries. There are several styles of gin, including distilled gin, compound gin, and London dry gin.

Irish Cream: A creamy liqueur made with cream, Irish whiskey, and other ingredients.

Licor 43: A bright yellow Spanish liqueur made with 43 herbs and spices and scented with citrus and vanilla.

Lillet: An aromatic aperitif wine from France. Lillet comes in two varieties: red and white.

Madeira: A fortified Portuguese wine that ranges from dry to sweet.

Manzanilla: A style of dry sherry made in Sanlúcar de Barrameda in Southern Spain.

Maraschino: A floral, bittersweet Italian liqueur made from bittersweet marasca cherries and their pits, and sweetened with sugar.

Orange Bitters: Cocktail flavoring made from the peels of bitter oranges and other herbs, spices, and botanicals.

Ouzo: An anise-flavored aperitif consumed in Greece and Cyprus.

Parfait d'Amour: A floral liqueur known for its purple hue.

Pernod: An anise-flavored liqueur that sometimes serves as a substitute for absinthe.

Peychaud's Bitters: Aromatic bitters that are bright red, invented in New Orleans in the 19th century.

Pisco: Un-aged brandy distilled from Muscat and other grapes in Chile and Peru.

Rum: A distilled spirit made from fermented sugarcane juice, ranging from light to dark.

Schnapps: A grain spirit that is usually mixed with flavors, sugar, and glycerine. Some of the most popular flavors include butterscotch, peach, cinnamon, and sour apple.

Sherry: Fortified white wine made in the Jerez region of Spain.

Sloe Gin: A red liqueur made from the sloe plums of the blackthorn bush, and is actually not a gin at all.

Southern Comfort: An American liqueur flavored with peaches and made from a whiskey base.

St-Germain: An elderflower liqueur redolent of pear, peach, lychee, and grapefruit.

Tequila: A Mexican spirit made from the blue agave plant.

Triple Sec: A colorless orange-flavored liqueur made from the dried peels of sweet and bitter oranges and with flavors.

Vermouth: An aromatic fortified wine ranging in color, from red to white, and in taste, from dry to very sweet.

Vodka: A colorless and distilled spirit that is often flavored with fruit.

Whiskey: A spirit that is made from grain and cooked with water, which is then fermented and distilled.

Flirting

Drinks to Light a Spark

Flirtation: where every sexy encounter begins. A coy smile, a tilt of the head as you twirl a lock of hair around your finger, or even lightly resting your hand on his arm as you lean in closely to listen. Something as subtle as gently recrossing your legs as you straighten your skirt or looking into someone's eyes can communicate a spark that will raise your temperature, make your heart beat a little faster, and make you feel a little bit more alive.

Sometimes things go further.
Sometimes that's where it ends.
But no matter what,
flirting sure is fun.

Raspberry simple syrup gives this slightly citrus and anise gin cocktail a bit of rosy color, much like the pink blush that creeps into the cheeks of a young lady when she gets excited. Who's to say why she's blushing?

Maiden's Blush

2 ounces dry gin

¾ ounce lemon juice

1 teaspoon absinthe

1 ounce simple syrup (page 13)

1 to 3 dashes raspberry syrup (page 13)

Lemon wedge, for garnish

Shake the gin, lemon juice, absinthe, and simple syrup with ice in a cocktail shaker. Strain into a chilled cocktail glass. Top with raspberry syrup and garnish with a lemon wedge.

Fluffy Ruffles

The name refers to the fluffy ruffles that adorned women's petticoats when this drink was invented in the early twentieth century, but it also evokes images of a flirty slip peeking out beneath a sundress, or a bit of **sexy lingerie** visible beneath your dress if you stand in just the right light.

Consider this cocktail the Manhattan's girly sister, substituting white rum for rye and feminine charm for brawn; it's like the younger sister her brother's friends can't stop staring at.

1 ½ ounces white rum

1 ½ ounces sweet vermouth

Stir the ingredients with ice in a mixing glass. Strain into a chilled cocktail glass.

Adonis

Adonis was the original hot young thing, so fine that all the ladies fell in love with him. Aphrodite saw him first, but after Persephone laid eyes on Adonis, she refused to give him back. Can you imagine the **cat fight** that ensued? Zeus had to be called in to settle the argument.

Made with sweet vermouth and dry sherry, this cocktail is perfect as an aperitif, preferably sipped before dinner with your own hot young thing.

2 ounces dry sherry

1 ounce sweet vermouth

Dash of orange bitters

Maraschino cherry, for garnish

Stir the ingredients with ice in a mixing glass. Strain into a chilled cocktail glass. Garnish with a maraschino cherry.

Spanish Fly

Potations made from the Spanish fly beetle are believed to be some of the

world's oldest aphrodisiacs

—and also the most deadly. This strong, sweet cocktail has a similar effect. Proceed with caution: there's a reason the real Spanish fly is illegal in most countries.

1 $\frac{1}{2}$ ounces tequila
1 $\frac{1}{2}$ ounces Licor 43
Ground cinnamon, for garnish
Cinnamon stick, for garnish

Build the ingredients over crushed ice in an old-fashioned glass. Garnish with ground cinnamon and a cinnamon stick.

hanky panky

This classic drink was created by Ada "Coley" Coleman, the first head bartender at the Savoy Hotel in London, to impress actor Charles Hawtrey when he was seeking a drink with "a bit of punch." After one sip of this cocktail he drained the glass, exclaiming, "By Jove! That's the real hanky panky!"

A whisper of the super-bitter Italian amaro Fernet Branca gives this cocktail a bit of juice. Use as directed, to give your sexy encounters a bit of punch.

2 ounces gin
1 ounce sweet vermouth
$\frac{1}{4}$ ounce Fernet Branca
Orange twist, for garnish

Stir the ingredients with ice in a mixing glass. Strain into a chilled cocktail glass. Garnish with an orange twist.

Cuban Passion

✦ **White rum,** passion fruit, and fresh orange juice make this fruity, tropical cocktail eminently sippable. It's exactly what you'll want to drink while making eyes at the hot lover you're hoping to take home from the bar.

2 ounces white rum

1 ounce passion fruit juice

4 ounces orange juice

1 to 2 dashes grenadine syrup,
   for garnish (page 12)

Lime wedge, for garnish

Shake the rum, passion fruit juice, and orange juice with ice in a cocktail shaker. Strain over ice in a highball glass. Float the grenadine on top. Garnish with a lime wedge.

Rated R

There comes a time in any flirtation when banter and body language transition from PG-13 to R-rated. Made with fruity, exotic, and the aptly named passion fruit, this cocktail slips down the throat with ease, making it ideal to aid that special transition.

2 ounces gin

1 ounce passion fruit puree

$2/3$ ounce lemon juice

Dash of passion fruit syrup (page 12)

Lemon twist, for garnish

Shake the ingredients with ice in a cocktail shaker. Serve on the rocks in a wine glass or goblet. Garnish with a lemon twist.

maneater

✦ If a Fluffy Ruffles cocktail is the Manhattan's girly younger sister, this drink can be considered his sexy cousin from the Big Easy. Strong and stirred and made with brandy, this drink packs a punch with a hint of sweetness and spice to soften the blow. Make no mistake, though, she's destined to take no prisoners.

1$\frac{1}{2}$ ounces Southern Comfort

1$\frac{1}{2}$ ounces brandy

1 to 2 dashes orange bitters

✦ Stir the ingredients with ice in a mixing glass. Strain into a chilled cocktail glass.

Sure, dirty martinis are a gateway cocktail for many, but in essence, they are little more than a big glass of vodka or gin filled to the brim with olive brine. There's nothing sexy about that.

This cocktail is a nod to the martini's roots that substitutes Manzanilla for vermouth, a sophisticated take on a drink often requested by cocktail virgins. More savory than a martini, more refined than a glass full of booze and brine, and a great recipe to teach the hot bartender you've been eyeing.

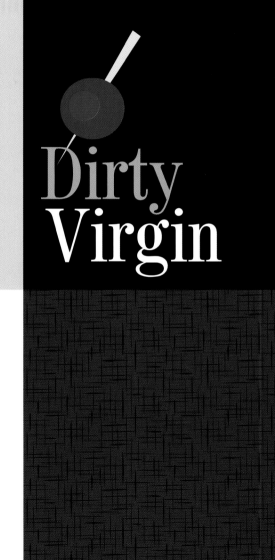

Dirty Virgin

2 ounces gin

1 ounce Manzanilla

1 teaspoon olive juice

Olive, for garnish

Stir the ingredients with ice in a mixing glass. Strain into a chilled cocktail glass. Garnish with an olive.

Aphrodite's Love Potion

Aphrodite was a smoke show. *Her beauty was so great,* the Greek gods feared it would cause jealousy among them and ultimately lead to war. They married her off to Hephaestus, who just couldn't keep her satisfied. She took many lovers, both gods and mortals. Aphrodite's love was surely sweet, strong, and not to be toyed with, much like this beautiful concoction.

$1\frac{1}{2}$ ounces brandy

5 ounces pineapple juice

Dash of Angostura bitters

Pineapple wedge, for garnish

2 maraschino cherries, for garnish

Build the ingredients over ice in a highball glass. Garnish with a pineapple wedge and two maraschino cherries.

Peep Show

A striptease is a striptease, but there's something decidedly retro about watching one through a tiny peephole that goes black when your allotted time is up. This could be the ultimate form of flirting, brushing right up close to a sexy encounter that's just moments away from fading to black. This shot packs a strongly flavored punch, much like its kinky namesake.

1 ounce Dubonnet	Shake the ingredients
1 ounce brandy	with ice in a cocktail
½ ounce Pernod	shaker. Strain into
½ ounce lime juice	a shot glass.

Gin and Sin

For many of us, these two already go hand in hand. Fruity and pink, this libation seems innocuous enough, but it's a potent potable. Consume several while in close quarters with your object of desire—and see how quickly the former begets the latter.

1 ½ ounces gin

1 ounce lemon juice

1 ounce orange juice

Dash of grenadine syrup (page 12)

Shake the ingredients with ice in a cocktail shaker. Strain into a chilled cocktail glass.

Hooking Up

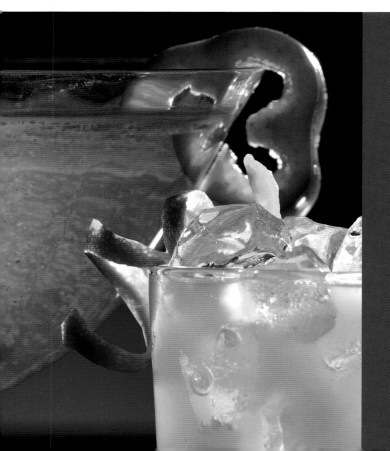

Drinks to Get You in the Mood

Few things are as much fun as a full-blown make-out session. When hours of flirting lead to palpable sexual tension, sometimes it feels like all you can do to keep your hands off someone. Patience, darling, patience.

Or not. A hot-and-heavy session outside a restaurant as it closes down, or in the elevator as you're going up, may very well make for

the sexiest moments of your life.

Over-the-Pants
Hand Job

Whatever happened to the hand job? Every once in a while it's fun to rock it like a couple of teenagers, jump into the back seat of a car, and go at it just like you did in high school. Or, if you have enough of these at the bar, you may even attempt to get things started under the table. No one ever has to know, provided he can keep his cool.

Needless to say, this drink is spicy and exciting, just like its namesake.

Cayenne sugar, for cocktail rim (page 16)

2 ounces gin

1 ounce spicy syrup (page 13)

$\frac{3}{4}$ ounce grapefruit juice

$\frac{3}{4}$ ounce lime juice

Rim a chilled cocktail glass with cayenne sugar and put aside. Shake the ingredients with ice in a cocktail shaker. Strain into the chilled cocktail glass.

Pink
Lace
Panties

A flirty drink requires a flirty name, much like this beverage. Of course, the color of a woman's panties is her business, but most of the time, guys are going to try to snag a glimpse. Will your outfit reveal a hint of pink? This might be exactly the thing to make the right gentleman weak in the knees.

2 ounces gin

1 ounce lime juice

$\frac{1}{2}$ ounce triple sec

$\frac{1}{2}$ ounce grenadine syrup
   (page 12)

Lime twist, for garnish

Shake the ingredients

with ice in a cocktail shaker. Strain into a chilled cocktail glass. Garnish with a lime twist.

BLU
NEGLIGEE

TRAIPSING AROUND IN A SHEER LITTLE SLIP

can sometimes be sexier than wearing nothing at all. There's a lot going on in this subtle-looking, liqueur-based cocktail. Mix one up after slipping into something a little more comfortable. Or better yet, stir one till it's ice cold as you wait for your lover to come over, then serve both at the door.

There's a reason why you see this kind of scene played out in sexy movies.

1 ounce green Chartreuse

1 ounce Parfait d'Amour

1 ounce ouzo

Stir the ingredients
with ice in a mixing
glass. Strain into a
chilled cocktail glass.

Leather and Lace

There's something undeniably sexy about a woman who can sport leather or lace, especially if she can get away with rocking both at the same time.

Crème de violette and Champagne lace this gin-based cocktail with a feminine, floral nose and taste. Any guy interested in the doll who orders this would be silly not to sip one, too.

2 ounces gin

¾ ounce lemon juice

½ ounce simple syrup (page 13)

½ ounce crème de violette

Dash of grenadine syrup (page 12)

Champagne, to top

Shake all ingredients except the Champagne with ice in a cocktail shaker. Strain into a chilled cocktail glass. Top with the Champagne.

Hickey

2 ounces vodka

1 ounce pomegranate liqueur

¾ ounce lime juice

½ ounce grenadine syrup
(page 12)

Pink Champagne, to top

Lime twist, for garnish

Shake the ingredients with ice in a cocktail shaker. Strain into a chilled cocktail glass. Top with the pink Champagne and garnish with a lime twist.

Hickeys are funny when you're in high school, but isn't marching around with one on your neck a little déclassé for a grown-up? Decidedly not, I say, if the make-out session was worth it. Wear it like a badge of honor as you sip one of these sweet, tart concoctions.

Between the Sheets

Yet another classic with a highly suggestive name, this

cocktail drinks very much like a Sidecar, minus the sugar rim, with a little dollop of

light rum to lighten and sweeten the deal. It's a little more feminine and summery,

and easier to drink without getting sticky fingers like its brandy-based cousin. A

few of these will no doubt guide you to the destination that the name suggests.

1 ounce brandy
1 ounce light rum
1 ounce triple sec
¾ ounce lemon juice

Shake the ingredients with ice in a cocktail shaker. Strain into a chilled cocktail glass.

Erection

Despite its name, this pink and fruity cocktail has all the trappings of a drink that's specially for the ladies. Made with fresh passion fruit, cranberry, and orange juices, it's sure to please any woman who orders it. If only every hookup were so easy.

$1\frac{1}{4}$ ounces 151 rum

$1\frac{1}{4}$ ounces passion fruit juice

$1\frac{1}{4}$ ounces cranberry juice

$1\frac{1}{4}$ ounces orange juice

$1\frac{1}{4}$ ounces spiced rum

Orange twist, for garnish

Shake the ingredients with ice in a cocktail shaker. Serve on the rocks in an old-fashioned glass. Garnish with an orange twist.

sex with the ex

do the jalapeño pepper, maple syrup, and cayenne pepper in this recipe make the drink seem like something you just shouldn't drink? Likewise, sex with the ex isn't always the best idea, but much like this cocktail, it can oftentimes be spicy, invigorating, and exciting.

or at least just once in a while.

1 jalapeño pepper slice, plus 1 slice for garnish
$\frac{1}{2}$ ounce maple syrup
$\frac{3}{4}$ ounce lemon juice
2 ounces Plymouth gin
Pinch of cayenne pepper, for garnish

Muddle one jalapeño pepper slice and maple syrup in a mixing glass. Add the lemon juice, gin, and ice. Shake the ingredients in a cocktail shaker. Strain into a chilled cocktail glass. Garnish with the cayenne and the remaining jalapeño pepper slice.

Silk Stocking

Silk Stockings strewn on the bedroom floor beneath a tangle of sheets can mean only one thing: someone had a good time taking them off.

Cream, crème de cacao, and Chambord tame the tequila base of this drink. But make no mistake: tequila was definitely involved in the removal of the stockings. It always is.

1 1/2 ounces tequila

1 ounce heavy whipping cream

1/2 ounce crème de cacao

1/2 teaspoon Chambord

Shake the ingredients
vigorously with ice in a
mixing glass. Strain into
a chilled cocktail glass.

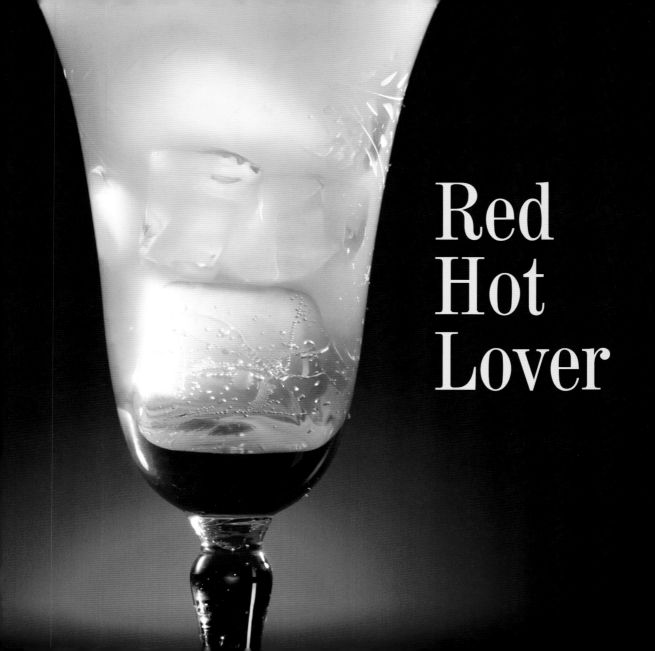

Red
Hot
Lover

Strong, sweet, a little exotic,

and easy to swallow—

who wouldn't yearn

for someone like that

for their next hookup?

This cocktail caters to

each of these whims

and is sippable enough

to drink all night. Sounds

absolutely perfect.

2 ounces vodka

1 ounce strawberry juice

1 ounce orange juice

½ ounce peach liqueur

Dash of grenadine syrup
    (page 12)

Shake the ingredients

with ice in a cocktail
shaker. Strain over ice
in a wine glass or goblet.

FRENCH KISS

IT'S THE FIRST AND MOST IMPORTANT STEP in any hookup, and your first way to tell if you've got chemistry. Like that first innocent exploration, this drink is sweet, soft, and subtle. Mint and Pernod add complexity, much like the kisses that follow—and then turn into a full-blown make-out session.

2 ounces gin

1 sprig fresh mint, plus a sprig for garnish

¾ ounce simple syrup (page 13)

¾ ounce lime juice

¼ ounce Pernod

SHAKE THE INGREDIENTS with ice in a cocktail shaker. Strain into a chilled cocktail glass. Garnish with the second mint sprig.

Second Base

St-Germain and grapefruit juice

work to make Pisco, the un-aged brandy base of this cocktail, sing. Both Peru and Chile lay claim to Pisco, and the topic of who makes the best is hotly debated between the countries. The definition of "getting to second base" is argued nearly as passionately in urban slang. Is it over the shirt or under the skirt? Is it Peru or Chile? After a couple of these, no one cares.

1 1/2 ounces Pisco
1 1/2 ounces St-Germain
1 1/2 ounces grapefruit juice
1 to 2 dashes Peychaud's Bitters

Shake the ingredients

with ice in a cocktail shaker. Strain into a chilled cocktail glass.

Hot and Heavy

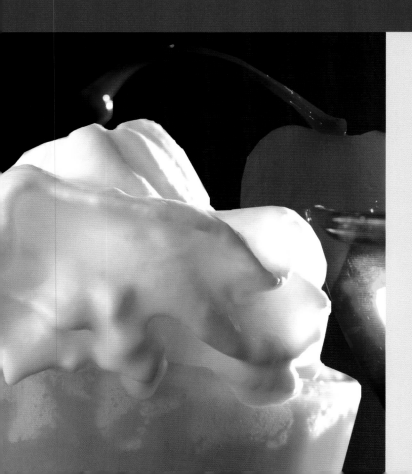

Drinks to Help You Get It On

You've finally made your way into the bedroom. Or, maybe you decide you're going to do it on the kitchen table. Or the couch. Wherever you are, once tucked securely away behind closed doors, you can finally let all your inhibitions go.

Drinks in this chapter describe how the hot-and-heavy makeout sessions can graduate from PG-13 to R- or X-rated. They feature explicit titles that describe unspeakable acts of naughtiness. Foreplay, really, with a bit of sultry kinkiness thrown into the mix. These drinks are meant to help you get it on.

Bosom Caresser

Another classic. It would be tough to order this drink for the object of your desire without raising their suspicions as to what you really want to do. So go with it. Egg yolk, a common ingredient in pre-Prohibition cocktails, serves to give this drink a smooth, creamy texture—exactly what you'd hope to find in a drink so appropriately named.

1½ ounces brandy
1 egg yolk
¾ ounce Cointreau
¾ ounce Madeira
¼ ounce grenadine syrup (page 12)

Dry shake the ingredients in a cocktail shaker for twenty seconds (page 14). Add ice, and then shake vigorously. Strain into a chilled cocktail glass.

WHIPS 'N' CHAINS

THIS DRINK is almost like a perfect Brandy Manhattan. Sip quickly enough and it won't hurt going down—but IT MAY JUST EXCITE YOU BEYOND BELIEF.

½ ounce absinthe

1 ½ ounces sweet vermouth

1 ½ ounces dry vermouth

1 ½ ounces brandy

SWIRL THE ABSINTHE

in a chilled cocktail glass, discard the absinthe, and set the glass aside. Stir the remaining ingredients with ice in a mixing glass. Strain into the chilled cocktail glass.

BLOW JOB

THE OBLIGATORY DRINK of every bachelorette party, this shot must be taken without using your hands. Practice, ladies. No woman should march off to her wedding night without knowing how to give one of these.

¾ **OUNCE COFFEE LIQUEUR**
¾ **OUNCE IRISH CREAM LIQUEUR**
WHIPPED CREAM, TO TOP

COMBINE OR LAYER

the coffee liqueur and Irish cream liqueur in a shot glass. Top with the whipped cream.

Pink Pussy

Bitter Campari is tempered by peach brandy and citrus-flavored soda in this low-alcohol sip. It's the kind of drink you can serve to your lover all afternoon and well into the evening. If he can handle it, that is.

1 ounce Campari

$\frac{1}{2}$ ounce peach brandy

6 ounces lemon-lime soda

Build the ingredients over ice in a highball or collins glass.

Great Head

Made with whiskey and applejack, an American apple brandy that tastes much like an apple-flavored whiskey, this drink is recommended for experts only, much as its name suggests.

2 1/2 ounces whiskey

3/4 ounce applejack

Dash of Peychaud's bitters

Maraschino cherry, for garnish

Stir the ingredients with ice in a mixing glass. Strain into a chilled cocktail glass. Garnish with a maraschino cherry.

Order it with confidence while out with the object of your desire, then drink it as if you owned it. Pretty soon, you'll own him.

LEG SPREADER

THIS FRUITY, TROPICAL CONCOCTION would be a perfect companion to poolside flirting, or a long day spent ogling hotties at the beach. Since it tastes completely nonalcoholic, you may find yourself in a deliciously compromising position before you know it. OOPS!

1 ounce coconut rum

1 ounce apricot brandy

1 ounce melon liqueur

1 1/2 ounces cranberry juice

1 1/2 ounces pineapple juice

Lemon-lime soda, to top

Pineapple wedge, for garnish

Maraschino cherry, for garnish

BUILD the ingredients over ice in a highball or collins glass. Top with the soda. Garnish with a pineapple wedge and a maraschino cherry.

Deep Throat

LAYERING THE INGREDIENTS IN THIS POUSSE-CAFÉ CAN BE AS TRICKY AS ITS EPONYMOUS TECHNIQUE. PRACTICE, PRACTICE, PRACTICE, AND WITH TIME AND PATIENCE, **YOU WILL BECOME AN EXPERT.**

1 OUNCE COFFEE LIQUEUR
1 OUNCE CHILLED VODKA
1 OUNCE HEAVY WHIPPING CREAM

LAYER THE INGREDIENTS IN A SHOT GLASS.

handcuffs are fun, but there's something to be said for tying some-one to the bedpost with a silk scarf, or even your stocking in a pinch. This fruity, tropical cocktail is just like that: more approachable, but equally naughty.

tie me to the bedpost

2 ounces vodka

$\frac{1}{2}$ ounce coconut rum

$\frac{1}{2}$ ounce melon liqueur

$\frac{1}{2}$ ounce lemon juice

$\frac{1}{2}$ ounce lime juice

$\frac{1}{2}$ ounce simple syrup (page 13)

shake the ingredients

with ice in a cocktail shaker.
Strain into a chilled cocktail glass.

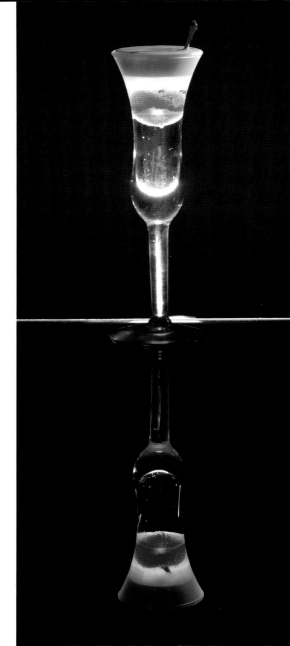

Angel's Tit

Yet another classic cocktail with a dirty name, the Angel's Tit dates from the Prohibition era. There is no question how this drink, made with sweet, floral maraschino liqueur and cream and topped with a strategically placed cherry, got its name. Sample one in place of dessert, before slipping off into the night.

1 1/2 ounces maraschino liqueur
2/3 ounce heavy whipping cream
Maraschino cherry, for garnish

Pour the maraschino liqueur into a shot glass.
Float the cream on top.
Garnish with a maraschino cherry.

Wet Spot

This drink was invented at a Manhattan bar famously named for the beds that lined its walls where guests imbibed. One can only imagine what might happen in such a place after too many of these. After all, any hot-and-heavy night is bound to leave a bit of evidence behind.

$1\frac{1}{2}$ ounces Plymouth gin

1 ounce apple juice

$\frac{3}{4}$ ounce lemon juice

$\frac{1}{2}$ ounce apricot brandy

$\frac{1}{2}$ ounce St-Germain

Lemon wedge, for garnish

Shake the ingredients with ice in a cocktail shaker. Strain into a chilled cocktail glass. Garnish with a lemon wedge.

cunnilingus

his department will definitely make

e ladies. This drink is a sweet, strong, stimulating shot

please any lucky lady who sips it.

1 ounce pineapple juice

½ ounce rum

½ ounce peach schnapps

Whipped cream, to top

Shake all ingredients except the whipped cream in a cocktail shaker.
Strain into a shot glass. Top with the whipped cream.

S&M

Espresso drinks play cruel but delicious tricks on the body: caffeine pushes your energy level up as the alcohol slows you down. For some people, a little cruelty is exactly what it takes to get really turned on. In that case, this aptly named drink may just do the trick.

2 ounces dark rum
1 ounce espresso
½ ounce coffee liqueur
½ ounce hazelnut liqueur

Shake the ingredients with ice in a cocktail shaker. Strain into a chilled cocktail glass.

hot pussy

this drink combines all kinds of heat into a glass: sweet, spicy cinnamon, peppery Tabasco sauce, and a fiery cayenne sugar rim.

your lips will probably burn after they touch it.

But who's to say you won't like it?

Cayenne sugar, for cocktail rim (page 16)
2 ½ ounces orange curaçao
¾ ounce cinnamon schnapps
2 drops of Tabasco sauce

rim a chilled cocktail glass with cayenne sugar and put aside. Stir the ingredients with ice in a mixing glass. Strain into the chilled cocktail glass.

BUTTERY NIPPLE

THIS DRINK APPEARS to be a relative of the Angel's Tit. Both are made with something creamy and something sweet, viscous, and aromatic. Can we consider these drinks their own X-rated category among the sours, fizzes, flips, and slings?

1 OUNCE BUTTERSCOTCH SCHNAPPS
2 OUNCES IRISH CREAM LIQUEUR

Pour the butterscotch schnapps into a shot glass. Top with the Irish cream liqueur.

All the Way

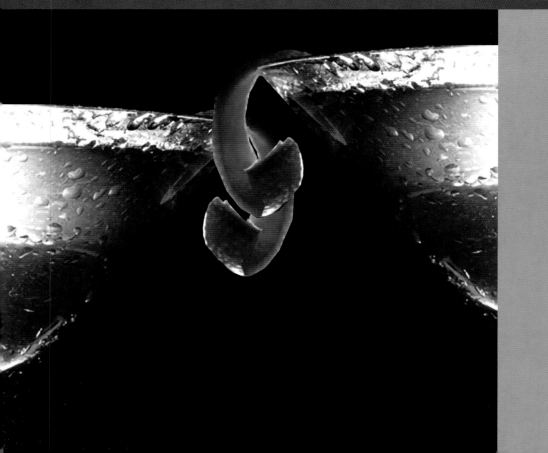

ks for the Climax

he kinky foreplay has

d once all the sensitive spots have been
y arrived at the moment you've been wait-
The drinks in this chapter are named for
noments leading up to the ecstatic release
Don't be shy. As you sip these drinks and
m a good omen for your sexual future.

climax many times

may they be as loud and proud as these

Ecstasy Cocktail

This cocktail is a relative of the Corpse Reviver (page 153). Both are equally delicious. Consider this tomorrow's hangover.

¾ ounce gin

¾ ounce blue curaçao

¾ ounce Lillet

¾ ounce lemon juice

Dash of absinthe

Orange wedge, for garnish

Shake the ingredients with ice in a cocktail shaker. Strain into a cocktail glass. Garnish with an orange wedge.

The Magnum

Applejack is a powerful ingredient that tastes much like whiskey on its own. Simple syrup, lemon juice, egg white, and soda water help tame this potent potable. Therein lies the name, The Magnum. It may be slightly intimidating, but it's certainly what we are always hoping for.

Go slowly, ladies. You'll be just fine.

1½ ounces applejack
1 ounce lemon juice
1 egg white
½ ounce simple syrup (page 13)
Soda water, to top

Dry shake the ingredients in a cocktail shaker for twenty seconds (page 14). Add ice, and then shake vigorously. Strain over ice in a highball or collins glass. Top with the soda water.

faster, faster

Lillet (an aperitif wine) and dry sherry (a fortified wine) temper the raucous gin base of this drink a tad. But don't be fooled. You may sip the first one like a lady or a gentleman, but don't be surprised if the second goes down quickly—and the third and fourth, as the name suggests, faster and faster.

1 $\frac{1}{2}$ ounces gin

1 $\frac{1}{2}$ ounces dry sherry

1 $\frac{1}{2}$ ounces Lillet

Dash of orange bitters

Orange twist, for garnish

Stir the ingredients with ice in a mixing glass. Strain into a chilled cocktail glass. Garnish with an orange twist.

Screaming Orgasm

Made with almond, coffee, and Irish cream liqueurs, this drink is sweet ecstasy in a glass, with a bit of vodka thrown in to make sure you scream . . . or just get good and drunk. It's not about what we want with this drink, it's about what we deserve.

$1/2$ ounce vodka
$1/2$ ounce amaretto
$1/2$ ounce coffee liqueur
$1/2$ ounce Irish cream liqueur

Build the ingredients in layers in a shot glass. Or shake them with ice in a cocktail shaker before straining into a shot glass.

Multiple Orgasms

It's everything a Screaming Orgasm offers–but more. Tequila ups the ante as the powerful base for this shot, and cream makes it richer and more intense. Not everyone can achieve such a feat, but everyone can try.

1 ounce tequila

$\frac{1}{3}$ ounce amaretto

$\frac{1}{3}$ ounce coffee liqueur

$\frac{1}{3}$ ounce Irish cream liqueur

$\frac{1}{2}$ ounce cream

Build the ingredients
in layers in a shot glass.
Or shake them with ice
in a cocktail shaker before
straining into a shot glass.

SCREAMING
MULTIPLE ORGASMS

It's the stuff great sexual legends are made of.

May we all experience this at least once with the right partner in our lifetime. Till then, let this sweet, rich shot get you in just the right mood.

1 ounce Irish cream liqueur

1 ounce orange curaçao

$\frac{1}{2}$ ounce Galliano

1 ounce cream

Build the ingredients in layers in a shot glass. Or shake them with ice in a cocktail shaker before straining into a tall shot glass.

Hot and Wet

Back in the day, a martini was a drink made with almost equal proportions of gin and dry vermouth. Over time, the amount of vermouth has shrunk, but if you've never actually consumed a large glass of gin with a sizable dose of vermouth, you are sorely missing out.

Here we add jalapeño pepper and a dash of Tabasco sauce to spice things up for a savory take on the original aperitif. Hot and wet. Who doesn't like that?

4 jalapeño pepper slices, plus 1
    for garnish
2 ounces gin
1 ounce dry vermouth
Dash of Tabasco sauce

Muddle four jalapeño pepper slices in a mixing glass. Add the other ingredients, including ice, and stir. Strain into a chilled cocktail glass. Garnish with the remaining jalapeño pepper slice.

Hot, Wet, and Steamy

If tequila is known for one thing in this world, it's for upping the ante. A healthy dose of Mexico's noble spirit adds a bit of heat to this cocktail, taking it from simply hot to hot, wet, and steamy. Take your pick—both are bound to fire you up.

> 4 jalapeño pepper slices, plus 1 for garnish
> 1 ounce gin
> 1 ounce tequila
> 1 ounce dry vermouth
> Dash of Tabasco sauce

Muddle the four jalapeño pepper slices in a mixing glass. Add the other ingredients, including ice, and stir. Strain into a chilled cocktail glass. Garnish with the remaining jalapeño pepper slice.

slippery dick

This cocktail goes down easy and smooth, delivering a blast of sweet, minty, almondy flavor. Layering can be tricky with some cocktails, but not so when working with the thick liqueurs in this well-lubricated concoction.

1 ounce peppermint schnapps
1 ounce amaretto

Layer or combine the ingredients in a shot glass.

Climax

Applejack, dry vermouth, citrus, and fresh grenadine hit all the right notes in this cocktail, making it sweet but not cloying, tart but not puckering, and strong but not rough. An exciting balance, just right in all the right places—and just **what you'll need to reach your climax.**

2 ounces applejack

¾ ounce dry vermouth

½ ounce lemon juice

½ ounce grenadine syrup (page 12)

Shake the ingredients with ice in a cocktail shaker. Strain into a chilled cocktail glass.

One-Night Stand

Drinks for When You'll Probably Never See 'Im Again

Could we write a sexy cocktail book

without dedicating a chapter to the one-night stand you'll never forget? We know you have had one. It's what made your business trip to Paris so steamy, or your vacation in Turks and Caicos hot and wild. You've been plenty kinky with your committed partners, of course, but there's something about knowing you'll never see that sexy cabana boy or hot Parisian chick again that can unleash a whole new, uninhibited you.

Was it the rum punch and island heat, or her irresistible inability to pronounce your name in her broken English? Who knows? Whatever came over you that steamy night, you were a different person, to whom

we raise a glass with these kinky cocktails.

Sloe Comfortable Screw Against the Wall

It sounds like a college kid just made this drink up, doesn't it? But the name is actually a nod to its origins: it's a hybrid of a Sloe Gin Fizz, Screwdriver, and Harvey Wallbanger, with a little Southern Comfort thrown in for good measure.

1 ounce sloe gin
1 ounce Southern Comfort
1 ounce vodka
1 ounce Galliano
½ ounce orange juice

Shake the ingredients with ice in a cocktail shaker. Strain over ice in a highball glass.

SEX 'N' HONEY

THIS COCKTAIL IS SPICY-SWEET, JUST LIKE YOUR ONE-NIGHT STAND,

AND EXACTLY HOW YOU LIKE YOUR DATES. YOU'LL REMEMBER THOSE TENDER HONEY-KISSED LIPS FOR DECADES.

2 ounces honey vodka

2 ounces pineapple juice

1 ounce amaretto

2 dashes cracked black pepper, divided

1 star anise, for garnish

COMBINE THE VODKA, pineapple juice, and amaretto with ice in a cocktail shaker. Add 1 dash of black pepper and shake. Strain into a martini glass. Garnish with the second dash of pepper and the star anise.

ménage à trois

Surprised yourself with this one, did you? Maybe it took a few drinks to get into the swing, but a ménage à trois is certainly a racy way to get it on. This is a surreptitiously strong concoction, a few of which will definitely help you throw all inhibitions to the wind.

1 ½ ounces dark rum
1 ½ ounces triple sec
1 ½ ounces light cream
Maraschino cherry,
    for garnish

Shake the ingredients
well with ice in a
cocktail shaker.
Strain into a cocktail
glass. Garnish with
a maraschino cherry.

Quickie

Quickies are short, sweet, strong, and to the point, just like this unfussy cocktail. Now get down to it—you haven't got much time, but a quick tryst is the only way to get sex with your hot one-night stand off your mind!

2 ounces gin

¾ ounce lime juice

1 ounce raspberry syrup (page 13)

Champagne, to top

Strawberry, for garnish

Shake the gin, lime juice, and raspberry syrup with ice in a cocktail shaker. Strain into a chilled cocktail glass. Top with the Champagne. Garnish with a strawberry.

Strip and Go Naked

It's a perfect recreational activity for you and your hot one-night stand. This punch is sweet, floral, a little feminine, and totally swiggable. **Imbibe it in large quantities,** and you may suddenly feel overdressed.

---

2 parts genever

1 part lime juice

$^1/_4$ part grapefruit juice

$^1/_4$ part maraschino liqueur

Fresh strawberries, for garnish

Mix the ingredients in a large bowl or pitcher.

Garnish with **floating strawberries.**

body shot

This drink is much more than the sum of its parts, thanks to the suggestive service style. Between the licking and the faux French kissing, it pretty much amounts to bar-friendly-foreplay-turned-drinking-game. Grab your dreamy one-night stand and get to it!

1 ounce tequila

1 packet salt

1 lime wedge

Pour the tequila in a shot glass and set aside. Find a willing partner, and choose a body part. The neck or stomach works best. Lick the chosen body part and pour the packet of salt on the spot you just moistened. Place a wedge of lime in their mouth with the skin pointed inward. Lick the salt off your partner, take the tequila shot, and then suck the lime in your partner's mouth. It doesn't get much more graphic than that.

SEX PANTHER

A tequila base gives this sorority-girl-tastic concoction a feisty little kick. Many people say drinking too much tequila makes them crazy. Your fling du jour should consider himself warned.

1 ½ ounces tequila
¾ ounce peach schnapps
¾ ounce Chambord
¾ ounce lemon juice
¾ ounce lime juice

Shake the ingredients with ice in a cocktail shaker. Strain into a cocktail glass.

Coffee liqueur, Irish cream liqueur, and milk sounds like a nightcap to us, but maybe that's the trick. Slip into a sheer negligee or your silk robe, turn on a little Marvin Gaye, mix up a couple of these, and *voilà*: sex machine.

sex
machine

1 $\frac{1}{2}$ ounces coffee liqueur
1 $\frac{1}{2}$ ounces Irish cream liqueur
1 $\frac{1}{2}$ ounces whole milk

Build the ingredients

over ice in a highball glass.

Sex Under the Sun

Feels so nice, you do it twice! If sex on the beach with your cabana boy got you hot and bothered, you may be something of an exhibitionist. Trot your one-night stand out in the daylight hours where you can get a good look at his rippling pecs. After all, you've got only so long to **play out this fantasy.**

2 ounces light rum

1 ounce dark rum

1 ounce orange juice

1 ounce pineapple juice

Dash of grenadine syrup (page 12)

Lime wedge, for garnish

Maraschino cherry, for garnish

Build the ingredients over ice in a highball glass. Garnish with a lime wedge and a cherry.

NYMPHOMANIAC

THERE'S SOMETHING TO BE SAID for a fling-style hookup with the right partner. With your pheromones working overtime, and a few rounds of these to get you going, you may just UNLEASH YOUR INNER NYMPHO.

2 ounces spiced rum
$\frac{1}{2}$ ounce peach schnapps
$\frac{1}{2}$ ounce coconut rum
Ginger ale, to top

SHAKE THE INGREDIENTS WITH ICE. Strain into a chilled highball or collins glass. Top with the ginger ale.

Sex on the Beach

With this drink,

it's all in the name: it conjures up images of hot, steamy lovemaking on a beach, perhaps under the stars, preferably with the aforementioned cabana boy you picked up in Turks and Caicos. A fantastic way to get laid—put it on the bucket list.

1 ½ ounces vodka

½ ounce peach schnapps

1 ½ ounces cranberry juice

1 ½ ounces orange juice

Build the ingredients

over ice in a highball glass

or goblet.

The Walk of Shame

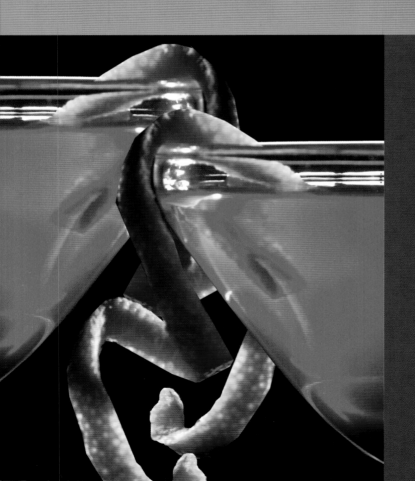

Drinks for the Morning After

Cocktails can be a cruel mistress.

Even the most teetotaling among us have had our moments: the sun rises, you wipe the martini haze from your eyes, and you see the world as a much less rosy place than it was before you passed out.

Then the morning doldrums set in, often accompanied by headaches, hangovers, and anxiety about those large blank spots in your memory of the night before. Hopefully you remember at least some of the fun that got you to this state. Either way, the drinks in this chapter are designed to take the edge off the morning after.

The morning after a wild night can find you in a state of disarray, from figuring out how to get home to wondering what exactly happened last night. Hush, hush, intrepid drinker. Think of last night as an exciting adventure and wash away your morning-after cares with one of these.

The Morning After

1 1/2 ounces gin
1/2 ounce St-Germain
1 ounce lemon juice
1 egg white
Lemon-lime soda, to top

Dry shake the gin, St-Germain, lemon juice, and egg white in a cocktail shaker for twenty seconds (page 14). Add ice, and then shake vigorously. Strain over ice in a high-ball glass. Top with the lemon-lime soda.

CORPSE REVIVER

THIS CLASSIC PRE-PROHIBITION COCKTAIL makes no bones about its function: to bring the drinker back from the brink of extinction when the dawn comes and the dark cloud of a deathly hangover begins to settle. It is also judiciously employable the night before the morning after.

3/4 OUNCE GIN
3/4 OUNCE COINTREAU
3/4 OUNCE LILLET
3/4 OUNCE LEMON JUICE
2 DROPS ABSINTHE

SHAKE THE INGREDIENTS with ice in a cocktail shaker. Strain into a cocktail glass.

If you had fun with your lover the night before, why would you leave without repeating the pleasure? Having an orgasm is a triumphant way to start the day. And if you manage to make it to brunch, sample this fruity concoction, which has enough juice to feel almost healthy.

Sugar, for cocktail rim (page 16)

1 ½ ounces light rum

½ ounce lemon juice

½ ounce orange juice

¼ ounce grenadine syrup (page 12)

¼ ounce orange curaçao

Rim a chilled cocktail glass with sugar and put aside. Shake the ingredients with ice in a cocktail shaker. Strain into the chilled cocktail glass.

Morning Sex

Afterglow
Fizz

Before there was the Bloody Mary, there was the Fizz, a drink usually containing egg white, soda, or some combination of the two, and consumed to take the edge off after a long night in the saloon.

You know what else takes the edge off? Morning sex. **Bask in its afterglow** with one of these.

1½ ounces gin

1½ ounces St-Germain

1½ ounces Aperol

1 ounce grapefruit juice

½ ounce lemon juice

½ ounce honey syrup (page 12)

Lemon twist, for garnish

Shake the ingredients with ice in a cocktail shaker. Strain into a chilled cocktail glass. Garnish with a lemon twist.

Wet Dream

Sometimes dreams are so vivid and exciting that our bodies can't help thinking they're real. What a disappointment to wake up and learn that the best sex you've ever had was literally in your head! There there. Sip one of these. It's bound to make you feel better.

2 ounces gin

½ ounce apricot brandy

½ ounce lemon juice

¼ ounce grenadine syrup (page 12)

Orange twist, for garnish

Shake the ingredients with ice in a cocktail shaker. Strain into a chilled cocktail glass. Garnish with an orange twist.

morning glory

urban slang holds several different definitions for the morning glory, none of which have anything to do with the cute blue flower that shares its name. One definition describes a guy waking up impressively hard. In another, a lucky guy wakes up to find his morning glory being well taken care of by the **oral skills of his adoring partner.** It's your call. Or just sip on the drink, which will refresh you no matter what its definition.

10 to 12 leaves fresh mint,
  plus a sprig for garnish
1 ounce honey syrup (page 12)
2 ounces Plymouth gin
$3/4$ ounce lemon juice
Coconut water, to top

muddle the mint

and honey syrup in a mixing glass. Add the gin and lemon juice. Shake the ingredients with ice in a cocktail shaker. Serve over rocks in an old-fashioned glass. Top with the coconut water and garnish with a mint sprig.

Walk of Shame/March of Glory

Walk of Shame: Shamefully trekking home in platform heels, last night's makeup, and a cocktail dress past joggers, professionals en route to work, and children on their way to school.

March of Glory: See above, replacing "shamefully" with "proudly." Yes, you can.

2 ounces vodka

1 ounce blackberry syrup (page 13)

¾ ounce lime juice

Fresh blackberries

Fresh raspberries

Ginger ale or Champagne, to top

Shake the ingredients with a few fresh blackberries and raspberries in a cocktail shaker. Strain over crushed ice in a highball or collins glass. Top with a splash of ginger ale. To make this a March of Glory, top with Champagne. Garnish with fresh blackberries and raspberries.

HOPE HE CALLS

2 1/2 OUNCES GIN
1/2 OUNCE EGG WHITE
1/2 OUNCE LEMON JUICE
1/4 OUNCE GRENADINE SYRUP
(PAGE 12)

DRY SHAKE THE INGREDIENTS
IN A COCKTAIL SHAKER FOR
TWENTY SECONDS (PAGE 14).
ADD ICE, AND THEN SHAKE
VIGOROUSLY. STRAIN INTO
A CHILLED COCKTAIL GLASS.

ONCE UPON A TIME,

women used to sit by the phone and wait for men to call. Now we have cell phones, text messages, e-mail, and Facebook—so many more ways to be blown off by a guy. Enough is enough! Pour yourself a stiff one of these. After one, he'll start to fade from memory; after two, you'll delete his number; after three or more, you just may have found someone else to lavish your attentions on.

FAVORITE MISTAKE

MADE WITH GIN, applejack, fresh lemon juice, and St-Germain, this foamy treat seems harmless enough, much like that little white lie you keep telling yourself about your favorite mistake. It's so wrong, but who can resist going back for more?

1 $^1/_2$ ounces gin

1 egg white

$^1/_2$ ounce applejack

$^1/_2$ ounce lemon juice

$^1/_2$ ounce St-Germain

Dash of orange bitters

DRY SHAKE THE INGREDIENTS

in a cocktail shaker for twenty seconds (page 14). Add ice, and then shake vigorously. Strain into a chilled cocktail glass.

What's Your Name, Again?

Waking up without knowing your one-night stand's name is just the worst. It takes savvy, skill, and a little bit of luck to figure it out and/or get out as quickly as you can. Proceed directly to the bar and order one of these. Depending on what you've just gone through, you may want to order it as a shot.

1½ ounces gin
1½ ounces lemon juice
¾ ounce orange curaçao
¾ ounce cherry liqueur
Lemon-lime soda, to top
Lime wheel, for garnish

Shake the ingredients

with ice in a cocktail shaker. Strain over ice in a chilled highball glass. Top with the lemon-lime soda and garnish with a lime wheel.

FORMULAS FOR METRIC CONVERSIONS

FORMULAS FOR METRIC CONVERSION

Ounces to grams=multiply ounces by 28.35

Cups to liters=multiply cups by .24

METRIC EQUIVALENTS FOR WEIGHT

U.S.	Metric
1 oz	28 g
2 oz	57 g
3 oz	85 g
4 oz ($\frac{1}{4}$ lb)	113 g
5 oz	142 g
6 oz	170 g
7 oz	198 g
8 oz ($\frac{1}{2}$ lb)	227 g
12 oz ($\frac{3}{4}$ lb)	340 g
14 oz	397 g
16 oz (1 lb)	454 g
2.2 lbs	1 kg

Source: Herbst, Sharon Tyler. *The Food Lover's Companion*, 3rd ed. Hauppauge, Barron's, 2001.

METRIC EQUIVALENTS FOR VOLUME

U.S.	Metric	
$\frac{1}{8}$ tsp.	0.6 ml	—
$\frac{1}{4}$ tsp.	1.2 ml	—
$\frac{1}{2}$ tsp.	2.5 ml	—
$\frac{3}{4}$ tsp.	3.7 ml	—
1 tsp.	5 ml	—
1$\frac{1}{2}$ tsp.	7.4 ml	—
2 tsp.	10 ml	—
1 Tbsp.	15 ml	—
1$\frac{1}{2}$ Tbsp.	22 ml	—
2 Tbsp. ($\frac{1}{8}$ cup)	30 ml	1 fl. oz
3 Tbsp.	45 ml	—
$\frac{1}{4}$ cup	59 ml	2 fl. oz
$\frac{1}{3}$ cup	79 ml	—
$\frac{1}{2}$ cup	118 ml	4 fl. oz
$\frac{2}{3}$ cup	158 ml	—
$\frac{3}{4}$ cup	178 ml	6 fl. oz
1 cup	237 ml	8 fl. oz
1$\frac{1}{4}$ cups	300 ml	—
1$\frac{1}{2}$ cups	355 ml	—
1$\frac{3}{4}$ cups	425 ml	—
2 cups (1 pint)	500 ml	16 fl. oz
3 cups	725 ml	—
4 cups (1 quart)	.95 liters	32 fl. oz
16 cups (1 gallon)	3.8 liters	128 fl. oz

Acknowledgments

Big thanks to all of the amazing bartenders who contributed cocktail recipes and inspiration for this book: Jen Fields, Adam Connito, Audrey Saunders, and Willy Shine and Aishe Sharpe. Also thanks to Courtney Bissonnette, John Lee Stoddard, and Greta Thomas for creative help naming these drinks. Without you, the Over-the-Pants Hand Job just wouldn't be possible. Thanks to Holly Schmidt for aligning me with this project and Allan Penn whose photographic genius turned these cocktails into works of art. Big thanks to the Running Press team who made this book so beautiful: my awesome editor, Jordana Tusman, and Corinda Cook, who designed the cover and gorgeous interior. Thanks to Christine Eslao, Jackson Cannon, Lauren Clark, Kate Palmer, Adam Lantheaume, Trina and Beau Sturm, Eastern Standard, Trina's Starlite Lounge, the Boston Shaker, and Dorothy's Boutique for your help with glassware and other accoutrements. Cheers!

Index